AF521876

POEMS & DAYS

POEMS & DAYS

MICHAEL HANNON

ISIS PRESS
SAN FRANCISCO

ISBN No. 0-931037-03-4

ACKNOWLEDGMENTS

Some of these poems have appeared in the following magazines and journals: *City Lights Journal, Bricoleur, Out of Sight, Kaldron, Bleating Hearts, New Directions* and in limited edition books from Peter's Gate Press, Solo Press, rainbow resin press, and Turkey Press.

Cover photograph by Sarah Calhoun

For my wife, Nancy Dahl

CONTENTS

PRELUDES

Now we are in the midst of reality,
insofar as the tarantula is concerned.

LAUTREMONT

THE SEA GAZER

To behold unbearable flowers
has been my recurrent fantasy and wish
meanwhile I await an invitation to love

Called down to witness God
in his loveless immortality
I am drinking the moon

Let innocents hold to their ignorance
The sea reveals nothing to a novice heart

I was not always like this—
remember now my several years of faith

Some element of truth removes me
Undone I prepare my heart for the shock of paradise

Be jealous of sorrows

We are hurt and crying in the wood
the night is brief
and permanence belongs to God

This generation singular for a lack of heroes
we do not mourn what we have had
but what we cannot have again

So a man walking all night
will take from his pocket a picture
and weep
will be found drunk in the streets
his situation compounded by arrest
and he will keep that picture
nor give up weeping

All things connect in our elements

There is in these lines something I must forget

We have all been children
and in fact lost

The women came later
and for all of them I've not forgotten one
and she is old
and wiser than poetry
who also knows
that there is in the world
a difficult wind—
the best and only wind for men

So we live for the promise
that the mind may revolt
to some stronger condition

But mostly we are weak with horror
at the soul that wants to swim up
through babies and marriage
through murder and religion
yet wisdom might come from that

There are desperate contentions

To walk with one's self
is to know a pained endurance

To ride in a chariot gilded with friends
is to be admired

All things connect in our elements

I am a sea gazer plain enough
watching the white boats ply nets
among the trembling fish

Beset by the strands of my own life
I am often in need of salvation

Nothing is what it seems
I have watched my beauties change
and to me nothing is safe

After an hour the room is changed
not so much by light
as by the entrance and dismissal of thought

What were we thinking of?
That the universe is well made?
That God is not absurd?

So you see what I mean

It is too early for me to take up
the history of the region
and consolidate my intimations

I have seen my beauties change
and I have forgotten paradise

Did I say at the beginning my wish?

The wind is in my face
I go blinded by the flowers

SOLAR FUR

I.

The naked body
is a fact
shouldering aside
those who object

running
to the nearest mountain

and waiting for air
fire
water

whatever comes down

All day long
the nameless horses
come down through the trees
and eat time out of my hand
with their funny tongues

their eyes
like dead planets

At birth everything is taken from us

Our souls fall out through new eyes
and are pulled to earth

We hear the mute plea of animals
the dream horses crossing shallow water
crushing the ice into tears

Everything learns to be measured in blood

Some days
our secret partners
get up and leave us

The sun is hiding
in the mountain lake

The moon is somewhere else
crying until she is empty

Down the road strongly
my self is walking away

In the rain of torches and ice
the archer's shaft
nails down the night

A sound of breaking crystal
as the moon soars to her place
and the owls are released

A special owl
the one allotted to poetry
dives through my chest
and eats the reasonable mouse

II.

A language of palms
soars from the throat

climbs over walls
and pelts our window
with dates

Tough fingers
pry open our eyes

We take up instruments
and the rooms are filled
with a longing for language

Our footsteps sound hollow
crossing the tiles
of enclosed patios

A sea of fine notches
has undermined our garden
with a hall of blind supports

We greet each other

With a grace strange to us
we assume a formal attitude of crisis

Trees burst their jackets of mica
and outgrow themselves
palms exploding with wild green fingers

The clouds take our plans
and expose them
as fragile monsters of hope

This day
this stream losing itself in shadow
is all we've ever had

Everywhere tonight
is filled with the cold apology
of rivers changing course

Palms guarding the streets of new cities
echo the heart-cry of abandoned stones
wounded by the shoulders of the moon

An unexpected wind rises

Each thing takes up its own life
under the surgical knives of the palms

III.

Death has raised in me
a little man of its own

one who will not be changed
by embraces

He stands under a stone
threading my life
through the eye of a needle

The secret of the moon
is burnt out by winter

a piece of inspired machinery
cured of its dreams

and I have a life
I do not always inhabit

a separate life
a steady life
on which the moon is printed

on which my body smiles
like a curious timepiece

So it goes

Time pursues the world
around its star

and in human fields
a resurrection of the obvious begins

From the garden
a tarantula steps into the sky
and exhibits his solar fur

IV.

Something draws near the laughter

Something unspeakable
dissolving in its source
the symbols of fire and myth

Already it shines
in the secret air of stones

There are no stones in the sky
and no victory

Let us say
there are no sentimental eyes

There is a vast machine
humming Beethoven
and walking on the waters

There is a memory of you
going away from the piano forever

I don't know who you are

But I know your sure passage
through the split sky of my ribs

Exactly as a heart
my song of you celebrates blood
and hallucination

Late at night we meet in a tree
and try to remember our original bodies

Dog Spring comes down the blue canyon
growling arrows

As pure as the absence of philosophy
he opens the sea

All my life has moved towards this hour
this disappointment flooded with light

CATECHISM

Credo quia absurdum.

TERTULLIAN

WHO MADE YOU?

God made me.

Space convulsed—primal atmospheres shaken by remorse
sprawled on the fallen planet sobbing for breath.

The sun making a face in the slime, the face gibbering
awe and Goddamned beauty, its love a hostage to fear—
there I stood, killing what I stood on.

WHY DID GOD MAKE YOU?

A jewel floated in the palm of His hand,
seas panicked there, ice scattered light,
clouds went over it polishing doves—
it was remarkable, but not quite finished.

A sacrifice was required, some thing
to perish utterly in the face of its beauty.
God manipulated one of the animals. Light
with a new twist pulsed in the forebrain—
now it was finished, and terrible.

He hurled it into space.

WILL GOD ALWAYS BE?

Vanishing through the act, undoing the embrace,
winding up the string, taking it all back—
God survives, but not as God exactly.

What a pair we will make in the next version of this poem—
He in his mob-cap of innocence, and I in my helmet of rage.

HOW MANY PERSONS ARE THERE IN GOD?

Imagine God, unstable in the blank skin of His singularity,
trying to imagine an authentic *two*.

Imagine a third thing imagining Him. This is a mistake—
anything might come out of the third.

WHAT DO WE CALL THE THREE PERSONS IN ONE GOD?

Men without women, their minds cracking on the unknown
heard God boast: *Father, Son, and Holy Ghost.*

What on earth is broken, is in heaven repaired,
putting right a world of wrong.
Self-made in this image they began to murder for it.

WHAT IS SIN?

Creating light which would all power lend
to uncreated soul, God paused and split this notion
to the ground, creating night. From now on there would be
meridians and degrees.

Soul, conceivable in a body thus defined, gained credence
though it were like to perish from God's wit.

WHO COMMITTED THE FIRST SIN ON EARTH?

They watched the sun and moon fall out of bed,
the fruit in the garden ripen, ripen and not fall.

They discussed the senseless condition.

Inevitably, they ate what was put before them—
she believing in it, he to confirm his suspicions.

Lust flung them in a ditch, one on the other.

Everything had changed, yet nothing had changed.
Their guilt, like their curiosity, was unassignable.

They took it on themselves.

IS THIS SIN PASSED ON TO US?

The stain on the ceiling over the marriage bed
is not the same one.
At night it leaves and another takes its place,
exactly the same, but not the same one.

WHY DOES GOD ALLOW SIN?

Given Sin the world begins in earnest—
people act and speak according to God's dream.
The flow of drama is various and uninterrupted.

Without Sin the film would stop,
burning from its center out to the edges
of a blind and disinterested light.

Sin is error, if you will, but no mistake.
Sin began the world and Sin can end it.

DID ONE OF THE PERSONS IN GOD BECOME MAN?

He felt the star in the knitting needle, cold and faint.
He felt His skin, fingers and toes.
He heard love flogging itself through the walls.

He suffered, and something told him that suffering
was just another witness who wouldn't be called.
Death was His one sure thing and He feared it.

The disguise was complete.

WHY DID GOD THE SON BECOME MAN?

To satisfy sin. To rewrite the script.
To scrawl the word COURAGE in desperate clay.

Here was a paradigm, a sacrifice thrown back
at God's face—its poem lost in translation.

HOW DID JESUS SATISFY SIN?

Who would master oblivion by the power of love
is here betrayed, abandoned, crucified,
but He has touched a chord in these people—
His name is a sword in their hands.

In the botched town at the foot of the hill
whores argue and throw dice.

WHAT DID BAPTISM DO FOR YOU?

I was born twice, once on a kitchen table
loud in the knowledge of death, and once
scalded by water from the font, my face in a trance.

Somewhere men in black were planning
my Confirmation, my Penance, my Eucharist.
I was an instrument, and today was the day
for sharpening instruments.

WHAT WILL CONFIRMATION DO FOR YOU?

Now am I a marked man brushed by dogma's corpse,
a soldier falling back from a Moscow in his heart—
or am I written in the very name that saves, scribed
in the breath on eternity's windshield?

There's a ghost in this room and a weird captain.
I am speechless at what goes on.

WHAT IS THE SACRAMENT OF PENANCE?

Maps treated with paraffin unfold in a downpour,
flashlights probe them for the way to the forest,
the death-camp, the ovens.

Somehow God and I are responsible for this.
We say so, our faces hidden from our faces, say so.

If you tore down the difference between us you would see
one blind figure sinking into the filth of its own absolution.

HOW DO YOU MAKE YOUR CONFESSION?

Bless me Father, for I have sinned.
Forgive my cynicism, forgive my book.
Forgive my petulance—it is late,
jackdaws spring to the heart's lip.

Forgive me, as I forgive you this unrequited hour.

WHAT DO YOU DO AFTER CONFESSION?

I am walking on the tombs set into the floor,
making a wedding tent with my autonomous hands.
Face down on my cowardice, I can see black candles
burning underwater, each held in the fist of a child.

I turn to the broken world.

TANTRA

MY MOTHER WALKED OUT

My mother walked out.
My mother pointed her shoe.
I clung to my mother.
Crude logic conned the knife.
I fell.
Filthy life swam up and kissed the sun.
I looked down at my feet.
The abyss was humming with milk and Jesus.
My mother pointed her shoe at the roof.
The roof caught fire.
I filled the cup of my birth.
I looked down at my feet.
Smashed rock pulled down the sky and seared it.
I mouthed a sentence.
Behind me the axe bit into the crucifix.
I was out but still holding on.
I switchbacked up the ridge looking for a hog.
I found it before it found me.
I ate it.
It was good bristly meat.
I looked down at my feet.
The sea went under a glacier.
The stars came out fighting for pieces.
The stars turned me inside out.
The stars filled my cells with water.
I couldn't go anywhere without the stars.
I heard singing in the house.
I heard someone crashing in the brush.
I felt the sun coming a long way off.
I followed the furrow my mother left.
The light ate the flowers.
I wanted to be good.

I wanted to make something.
The propeller lifted my mother's skirt.
I saw her meat.
It made me crazy.
They crossed my legs.
I had to crouch in the library.
I looked down at my feet.
The rattlesnakes ate the light.
I held the dead jockey in my arms.
I read Rimbaud.
I wanted to win.
I looked down at my feet.
The teacher was kissing a penis.
My mother pointed her shoe.
The school burned down.
I was frightened.
I wanted to swallow my mother's feet.
My mother said it didn't matter.
I looked down at my feet.
It didn't matter.
I woke up in the dark.
I went to my mother's room.
My mother wasn't alone.
I asked God not to take my mother.
God gave me an earache.
I screamed and screamed.
My mother held me.
My mother told me.
God didn't have any meat of his own.
I screamed.
The pain was unbearable.
The bone man came.

The bone man cut out the bad part.
It hurt my mother.
I looked down at my feet.
My mother spun the ego.
A coin hit the whiskey glass.
My mother baked the bread.
It came out funny.
I ate it.
It made me crazy.
My mother split the atom.
My mother danced in the air.
The people all turned black.
She said it didn't matter.
I wasn't sure.
I wasn't sure of anything.
I looked down at my feet.
The crowd swayed the boardwalk.
My mother was in a hurry.
I held my mother's hand.
She found the right man.
She took him into the mirror.
I looked down at my feet.
The boardwalk made holes in the ocean.
My mother came out of the mirror.
She was twice as beautiful.
She was alone.
I helped my mother put on her shoe.
I looked up her dress.
There was blood on her teeth.
The police were looking for my mother.
They didn't know where to look.
My mother was asleep on the ocean.

I looked down at my feet.
I pretended to be dead.
Somebody said the penis was God.
My mother got dark in the face.
My mother spoiled the harvest.
My mother got into the animals.
My mother made them swell up.
My mother turned over the horse.
My mother hid me in the ruined corn.
She plowed the starry field.
She rubbed her bottom in the wheat.
Twisters surrounded the small town.
Minnows leapt out of the preacher's bucket.
Catfish glowed in the dark.
My mother took one look at the river.
The river buried the storehouse.
The river carried off the pigs.
I looked down at my feet.
It was cold.
My mother ate all the blankets.
My mother got into the dog.
My mother made the dog sing all night.
My mother got into the television.
She made it talk sense.
My mother scattered the suitcase on the mountain.
The lingerie whispered to the moon.
My mother sent for the rat.
My mother sent for the rainbow snake.
My mother rubbed me with camphor.
My mother filled the kitchen with squash.
I looked down at my feet.
I couldn't believe what I saw.

I got drunk.
The moon went out.
The trees flew away.
I walked the black country road.
I found my father.
He was carrying a red ball of words.
He was old.
I took it from him.
I kissed my father.
My mother came down from the attic.
She was old.
She was very beautiful.
My mother kissed me.
I walked out.
I never looked back.
I looked down at my feet.

VENERATIONS

If there is veneration even a dog's tooth emits light.

TIBETAN PROVERB

FREE WILL

Letting go that plastic part of myself in a woman
that part I know will always return through the maze
a skinned knee in another generation or an amorous eye
hanging in the ruins of a now metropolis—

I feel as if falling through some medium more blest than air
and more forgiving than water falling down some tunnel in earth
the warm walls of which are painted the whole blood of creation
falling with death at the bottom and no rancor.

Is this the act of an individual?

FACES

I have been the slave of breast
limb and genital the rise and fall
of hip and breath.

Always it was the face
which overthrew my addictive spirit
the eyes which sent me away
the mouth that called me back.

The last thing I expect to see
is some kind of face.

POEMS AND DAYS

I am living these poems and days in order
to have lived them in some future hour
so that the secret eye pressed to my window
may glim some happiness and mortality
before my lights go weird and dim and out.

I am living in order that this perfect joy
stabbed down through woman forest and animal blood
may turn in gloomy ward or silent room and close
with sight of death's release to make a harmony
in darkening air.

SONG

You'd never know the problem of evil
had crossed those features so prepared by night
to catch the morning in repose. Never know
our shadow of disturbing love.

She smiles as if the mind in searching God
had left a face for God's repair.

Whenever she awakes a tree is singing
its strong song of axes of water carried uphill
to the unfinished world.

DESIRE

What I desire has nothing whatever to do
with the ultimate destiny of winged things
and may not be heard over evolution's roar
but I have seen the owl twice of late.
Once suddenly white in the headlight's gaze
and once perched at the side of the road—
swollen oracle of feathery horn.

I take this to mean that I may yet learn
to live quietly wanting nothing from the light
wanting nothing from the darkness.

SONG

Mother sister beautiful companion of the night
again and again you wound me kiss me heal me
and try to say that because nothing is held
nothing can be lost.

Often I feel that I am only
the clarity of my pain held aloft
like a verse not to be spoken.

Mother sister beautiful companion of the night
keep playing please that deliberate music
which binds me to the dream of your free body.

MAYA

A transparent animal hacked into sections and labeled: WINTER
weather bent round the earth and sky like a work-grimed thumb
operas of cloud at forty thousand heart-stopping feet
feet and hands nailed to the earth the sorrow of many come down
to the one freezing ditch.

This wind keeps traveling from me to you
across the grinning perfect bones of maya.

ORIGINAL SIN

Finding out where God leaves off and we begin
is going to wear out our shoes.

There are galaxies where everything is down backwards because
the heart has touched zero. There are galaxies that don't exist.

Even the idea of stone is a baby in the story of walking
one foot in the dream of another.

BIRD LIKE A WOMAN

Snowy egret white tine of the marsh
standing all day in back bay water turning the air white.

At evening you become an old woman
and shouldering your sack of crabs and fish
walk away to a driftwood shack in the dunes.

Late at night cries from the cauldron
remind you of the Tao the fire and the darkness.

LIKE FATHER LIKE SON

The failure of my father's mind at eighty-six
adds itself to the wheel of sorrow almost gently.
If only it brought some brute peace in its wake
instead of these half-formed hatreds and suspicions.

I drive the coast road where a solid wave of faces
hack wings from vertical rock and hawks whistle
across the edge on a wrong-sided knife.

That night I awaken suddenly, crying out for the truth.

THE EDGE

The edge is where we stand and it is terror
to think of giving one's self over to that rip
torn from the bowel of rock.

Terror, the monstrous beauty of being
in the world of the world and yet
curiously undermined by staggering divisions.

Terror, to follow nothing into a horse,
a tree, a star, a child,
to couple with a woman who is like the sun,
to see the self moan and fall back broken.

It is intolerable, this always looking down
at the death of dreams and wholeness, knowing
you cannot rise and you will not fall.

BURNING BRIGHT

I am thinking with the other cells tonight
those blue ones just beyond the central fire
wheeling rim to rim in ecstatic matrix and oblivion

This is the seizure worth waiting for
the line between the lines falling from its book
into the furnace of notions—evil and beauty
burning bright.

This is where the starry mannequins take off their clothes.
This is where I stroke the knees of the stone ballerinas.
This is where poetry meets ignorance head-on. A crossroad
with someone dying of blood in at least four directions.

THALASSA

A drum is marching in the table.
For forty years the inanimate sustains an illusion of form
but each morning the sea knocks at the window.
The sea wants my last word.

When I leave the door is another cherished thing kicked shut.
An immense contradiction throws everything it has at my face.
Small steps one at a time go on without me.

SONG

Small chance that song might serve our wound—
love set against itself unnaming love calls out
for fire and blood.

The star between paired dreams explodes on time,
on time the shielding veil is rent, and we are atoms
turning in the light from another world.

Dishonored God, white heart in the white field—
what will you set against divided faith and loss?
Night's bitter symmetry? Love gorged on love?

Or will you take us from this howling age
up to an emptied pole wherein we may peruse a face
that's frozen self to self?

Difficult God, carnal heart circling with roses
in the false dawn of countless outpourings—
spare us the rhetoric of will.

FABLES

WHAT THE TIGER SAID

The night is vast.

Behind the walls of your room
you and I are living a powerful dream.

WHAT THE OWL SAID

When the earth quakes
listen to me, holding on
deep in the pines.

WHAT THE MOUNTAIN LION SAID

Concerning snow and eternity
I lecture to the lamb.

WHAT THE RACCOON SAID

I am the poet of midnight.

My shiny black hands
would like to crack the moon.

WHAT THE MOON SAID

When I broke away from the earth
I left a love charm
in that old tree down by the river.

Take her there, tonight.

WHAT THE CROW SAID

Though friendly to magic
I am not a man disguised as a crow.

I am night eating the sun.

WHAT THE ROSE SAID

I am the sea cut and folded.

I am the last evening
fallen on an enchanted shoulder.

WHAT THE RIVER SAID

Deep summer.

Both arms full of willows
I fall onto fields of light.

WHAT THE MOLE SAID

I hate the sun,
all that commotion.

I want to grind steadily
at the roots of darkness.

Work is my salvation.

WHAT THE GRASS SAID

Abjure despair.

We will raise children
in the spent lantern of your skull.

WHAT THE CICADA SAID

I am Pharoah
come from the land of the dead.

This is my last incarnation—
one long afternoon outside the window of a fool.

Michael Hannon was born in 1939. For over twenty years his poems have appeared in magazines, journals and anthologies both here and abroad. Prior to Poems & Days, *Michael's work has been collected in chapbooks and collectors' limited editions. Michael lives with his family in Morro Bay, California.*

Poems & Days
*was designed by Richard Rawles
and printed by Braun-Brumfield in
Ann Arbor, Michigan.*

Also by Michael Hannon

Solar Fur
A Door in the Water
My Mother Walked Out
Ship Without Paper
Venerations & Fables
Towards a Theory of Ignorance
Slender Means